HERE I AM

Ron Griffin

Here I Am

Ron Griffin

CITI OF
BOOKS

CITIOFBOOKS, INC.
3736 Eubank NE Suite A1
Albuquerque, NM 87111-3579
www.citiofbooks.com
Hotline: 1 (877) 389-2759
Fax: 1 (505) 930-7244

Ordering Information:
Quantity sales. Special discounts are available on quantity purchases by corporations, associations, and others. For details, contact the publisher at the address above.

Printed in the United States of America.
ISBN-13:   Paperback   979-8-89391-238-8
             eBook   979-8-89391-241-8

Library of Congress Control Number: 2024916023

RON GRIFFIN

I have been working for an oil company for 38 years, and I have been able to minister to God's children in almost every state and six countries. I have never asked for money or offerings because the gospel should not be bought; it is free because Jesus paid the ultimate price on the cross. I have lived the last 48 years of my life trying to obey the Lord in every way without asking for sacrifice.

This book I have written tells of my life and obedience to God as a young boy coming into a world of sin and degradation, and how I have been able to keep the strength to carry on through it all. I hope that others will read the book and be encouraged to read the Bible, because it is your love letter from God, who loves all His children and is preparing to come and deliver them into His great love for everlasting joy and peace like we have never seen. Selah.

One day, I sat out in my front yard, and a thought came to me that I needed to talk about experiences in my journey in this world as I have been for seventy-one years and moving on. I had been praying for the Lord to give me the wisdom I needed because I just didn't know where to begin with the thoughts to start writing.

So, I said, "Here goes," and this is the legacy of my life. I was born in this world in 1950. My mother released me into the world from the water in her belly. I came forth, and God breathed life into me, and I was alive for the first time upon this earth. I now am flesh and spirit alive. If we ever could really understand this birth, we would have all we need. God chose me, and now here I am in a new world and time I know nothing of, and they call me a baby. As I am to be in flesh, I begin to reason and think and grow. As my growth begins, I begin to get where I see, feel, touch, and even begin to learn what is all around me in this new world I am in. I remember, the very first thing I experienced in this world was death. So, I came into this world, and at three years of age, my grandfather had died, and I watched as they carried his body right by me. As time went on, I don't remember anything else till I was about five years of age. I was walking in the yard, heading toward a church on the ground. There was a stick I reached down and picked up, and I was going to show it to my mother, but she screamed at me to throw it down, and she said it was a snake. So, I put it down and went on to her. My next memory came at seven years old when I went to school. On my first day, I was excited. Everything went real; even I was having a great time meeting other kids my age. When the bell rang, I headed outside with other kids. It was my morning break, but I decided I was going home. I got home and told Mom school was out for the day. It was the first lie of my life. I wasn't at all sure why, but she said it was okay.

My mother worked in a restaurant in town, and I went there to see how one day I noticed how Black people could not eat with us and had to go to a backroom. I remember getting really angry with the owner, but then I calmed down. I begin to notice how kids made fun of me and asked, and I finally realized why; they told me I was crippled. I had no knowledge of that world. Then I was told I had to have surgery and wear iron braces because I had polio, and I contacted it at nineteen months old. they came out with a vaccine two years later. I guess it was time now for me to grow and to really learn what this new world was like to really see now my new journey that has been chosen for me since the beginning of time I wonder what was next for me, as I realized now as I was growing in this new body, how it was going to be very challenging and difficult for me because I was different. I remember when I would be called Chester and hop along gimp and all sorts of names, even though I didn't understand why the boys and girls were saying those things about me just because I had a limp when I walked. I've seen all life begin; it resurrected before me. I knew I was different and was not like anyone else on this earth. God had given me an opportunity to have a new life in this world. He made me special and different because of my faithfulness and obedience at the first age, and I began a new journey to be what he put me here for. Now as I began school, I would see many different people, colors and races of people. The next thing I remember was when I was about ten or eleven.

I experienced playing football and baseball, but I could never run because of my leg; but they made me a right guard because I was strong and hit hard. I really enjoyed playing baseball. It was very good, but I just could not run so I could knock that ball out of the park easily, so they had boys run for me. I guess it was embarrassing to me, so I quit and never played again.

As I moved on with my journey in this life, I began to notice in me more and more of the feelings for others that I was having, like what I saw in the first part of this journey of life, and it all began to make sense.

Remember the snake? That was my first reaction to good and evil since I was three or four years old. I carried that thought all my life. What if the snake had bitten me? That would have ended this journey of life. But good came; and through the scream of my mother, my life began that day. I guess, in all I've seen and thought growing up, I could do anything I wanted to do and not even be hurt. But boy, as time went on, it began to get very exciting.

Now the story of the past is a touch of my life as accurate as I can remember. I was raised up in a small town, and I never had much to do, so I began to seek others in my town and school to hang out with. I remember this boy, and his name was Jonny. We became great friends, and he was a lot of help to me because I now knew what a friend was. Then there was another boy who I became friends with but not as good as my friend Johnny. And then there was Terry. We were three amigos for all the time I was in this town.

In about 1960, we were told by my stepdad we were moving. I didn't like that because I was going to have to leave all of my beginnings. I was in my room one day, and I felt such a strong desire come over me that things just were not right in my life. So, I went across the street and walked up to a church, and I went in and sat down in the front, looking at the pastor, and I didn't see anyone, but I heard a voice say, "Here I am." I started to cry, and the pastor said, "Come and be baptized." So I went, and he sprinkled water over me and told me I was saved. I had no idea what he was saying, but I did hear that voice, and I knew it was my Father who had sent me on this journey. I told Mom and all my family about what had happened, and they just said that was good. Now the journey in my life started to take place, and I discovered a girl and began to want to know her. I felt what I thought was an amazing difference I have discovered for the first time in this world. I don't remember a lot about the relation, but it was different. But one day, I was told her whole family was killed in a car accident. I was about twelve or so.

The next few weeks were really hard for me to understand as we began to pack and get ready to leave for another town down in the valley. I would like to back up a little and say I also had two brothers from my earth mother, and they both were very different from me, and they never cared much for me. Even though we all came into this world the same way, we are all totally different, and I now understand what God meant. Many are called but few are chosen. If you think about it, we never had any choices if you are chosen by God. Everything in our journey has been set in place for us up to now in this journey of my life.

We now are beginning to travel a lot and live in different towns and meet all sorts of people. At twelve years of age, this was not easy on me. But I went, just as I was destined to do. I went out in the world that was really strange and scary, and I never realized what was going to happen. But as I began to grow, I realized I had nothing to fear. All my needs were being met. Now at fourteen or fifteen, we had moved to another state to start junior high and was asked to play football. I was so very excited about playing. I was told couldn't play because the school insurance would not cover me. I just let it go and forgot about it, even though it was another great disappointment in my life journey. So, I just moved on in my life. But more was coming, and it was beginning to see the real purpose of life. I remember how, all of a sudden, I was being tested by fear and intimidation in school by a bully all year in my first year in junior high school. I never had been in any type of scuffle with anyone, so I really didn't know how to handle the situation. The boys were much bigger than me, so I guess I was afraid to defend myself. I took a lot of bullying till my last day of school for the week and my last day of year to be going to school before we moved. He came up to me and slammed my locker, and I turned and hit him in the nose, and blood went everywhere. I felt so good about what I had done and felt sorry for him, and I almost cried. But I held back because I wanted to let everyone see I was not afraid of these bullies. The year of this school was over with, so we were out for summer, but I left and went to Alabama to stay with my grandparents and to see my biological dad. He was a bad drinker, and so was my grandfather. My grandma was a pretty good woman to deal with both of them. We got a call one day, and she told me to go with her to get him. When we got there, he was lying on the floor and was very drunk. My life was starting to get worse all the time and really didn't know what to do. I was so out of place in this new time in this journey

All this I had never seen in my time and this life. I just wanted to get back to my old life, but I had to stay there for a while. All the time, I remembered all the peace I felt the day I heard "here I am" in that soft voice just a few years back. And now all the I have been going through was taking tomorrow a toll on me. I decided I had seen enough, and it was time for me to go home. My parents had moved to Jackson, Mississippi, and I was starting school in a

few days. I was going to be in the tenth grade, I think, and it was to be my next journey in this world. I had been in about eight or nine different schools by this time in my life.

The longest I spent in any school was one year, from first grade to twelfth grade. I also, in these years, experienced a lot of History in some of the places I lived. I had a big playground in Vicksburg. We lived right next to Battlefield Park where the battle of Vicksburg was fought. I experienced so many horrible things in Mississippi. There was so much hatred for Black people. Robert Kennedy killed and John Kennedy.

Moving on to my new journey, I learned to be caring and compassionate about other people; I guess because of the polio I've seen everything differently than everyone. I could never hurt anyone. I was brought up in that little town, and it was all I knew up until now, the last couple of years of my journey. So now I was back home with my family. I was starting off in another school and beginning to make friends. Mostly now it seemed to be girls were my main focus. I had never been with a girl on a date until now, and I was taking a girl to a prom who was a little older than I was, but she asked me to. At that time, I had started smoking a little to fit in with the other kids. So, when we got to the prom, I lit up a cigarette, and she totally came loose on one and told me she would not go with me. So, I left and came home and didn't know how I was going to explain. This hurt me very badly because I didn't mean to hurt the girl, and it broke my heart. At this time, I was about as close to sixteen and really took a blow from my incident, and I said I would not do it again. She just didn't care, and that hurt even more.

As I began to progress in my new world, I would experience lots of small things that I had to learn to overcome, and it made me stronger. I was learning now after I got settled in our new town. I began to start finding places to go and meet people when I wasn't in school. I met a few guys who were musicians, and I tried to learn to play guitar. I was having a great time watching them play, even though I was good enough to play with them. By this time in this journey of my life, I was in the tenth grade, and I was a very outgoing person, but I just didn't fit in. I had long hair, and the school just didn't care about it. So, I got three days suspension several times because I was now developing into a rebel. This was a new thing for me, but it was all purposed for my life journey, so I had to take what came and reap what I sowed.

At about seventeen, I quit school and decided I was going to work. So, I set out on a journey to get a job in another state. So, I took off the Indiana. I don't remember who I went with, but I went to my first real job in this life journey. My mom and stepdad let me go and never tried to stop me at all. I was kind of shocked about that, but I went to work. I built towers for an Elec. Co. in Indiana. I worked and lived there for about six to eight months. I was walking down the street one night in Greensburg, Indiana, and saw a tree growing on the top of the courthouse; and that was really not a thing to see. Now I was in a world that I never had experienced, and I had money to spend and a life to live. I was truly on my own. I had a place of my own which I had shared with a couple guys I worked with, but I was really seeing what life was all about.

I got out there in this world even though I didn't know why I did the things I did, until I realized I was falling into the deep pleasure of this new life I was in. I began to get thoughts in my mind I was not used to and passions that were wrong, but I didn't know what sin was. So, once I realized what was happening, it was making me feel really bad. I knew I had to get out. I was with some of the guys one night, walking down the street, and a car drove by. A girl asked me if I wanted a date. So, I went with the people. There was another couple, and she was by herself. So now another temptation came over me, and it grabbed me. I was not prepared to play with this sin; so, like a snake, it bit me because I liked it.

I was tired of these things going on in my life. So, as I was getting ready to get out of this life, I was in a bad car wreck. The car went off a bridge and was turned upside down. I pulled everyone out of the car. They were all hurt badly, but I only had a scratch on my foot. I heard a voice, the same voice I had heard when I was that little boy, and said, "Here I am. You will get through. I didn't want to be around this life anymore, so a friend I had met said he wanted to go to Mississippi. So, we loaded up a headed to Mississippi. We went to

Jackson. When we got there, my family had moved to Alabama, so I had nowhere to go and no money, just my clothes. I started to look for a job, and I got a job at carnival. It was just setting up, and we went there, and I started to work building the rides. I was by myself now. The boy with me went back to Indiana. After we were finished building the ride, the boss asked me to stay and run the ride as long as I wanted. This was pretty cool. I was a seventeen-year- old who had never seen or experienced anything like this before, and I grew to know and understand people who were totally different. They were called freaks. In reality, these people were my real beginning into this next step into my journey. There was no one making fun of each other, and everyone just helped each other to make it. Sometimes it was hard living under my ride, taking baths in a horse stall and keeping dry and warm. So, at seventeen, I knew there was no way I could have gotten a job because of polio. So, I made the best of it as I could. I made four shows in the US with them, and the carnival would go down for winter.

So now it was time for me to move on in this journey. So now, after the experience of death and living in these eighteen years of my life, I moved on. So now I went back home to my little town in Texas where all this past life started and to the next journey in this part of God's awesome plan for me. I only had the clothes on my back, and I headed to Texas hitching rides. I took like forever because I looked pretty rough. My hair was below my shoulder, and it seemed when I got close to the south, I was being made fun of; they even tried to cut my hair, so I had to try to keep them away. I pulled a lot of bluffs because I was strong, and I made them get away without a fight. I finally made it to Texas and found that my mother and family were in Alabama. So, I went to Alabama and stayed for a little while to see my family, and I got in some trouble.

I started to experiment with LSD a couple times, and I really got scared of what I was going through. So, I left again and came back to Texas on a bus. I guess you would say I was becoming as man in this flesh, and all things I see now are totally different by the life I lived for the last eighteen years. I had no idea what I was going to do, but I went to Texas and stayed a while with my uncle, and I thought about finishing school. So, I went to night school. I only needed three credits in Texas to graduate. So, I started night school and worked at a gas station till one day I received a letter from the US government saying I had been drafted. I was to come to Houston for three days. So of course, if you are drafted, you have to go. I told them they were wasting my time there because I had polio.

The officer got mad, and I did also. He told me to take this written test and bring it to him. So, I was angry, and he and I just didn't think the same even though he was just doing his job. It was an easy test, but I just went down making true or false questions. When he saw what I had done, he got very mad and told me I was in the army.

When I went to take the physical, the doctor told me I should not have been there and to go home. So, they put me on a bus. I tried to get to work when I got back home, and I couldn't. I read in the newspaper about a job at a fab shop. I went, and they hired me. I only worked a couple weeks, and he laid me off.

I went to work selling magazines. I flew and traveled to several states. I finally left the road and went to West Virginia, and I met a girl on the road, and we liked each other. So, we wound up getting married. I really don't know why, but it didn't last. I worked at a plywood plant until I was fired because I was sick, and she never called in for me, and she became a very unstable person. But it was my fault because I spent all my time working, and she stayed home. I went to work offshore with my cousin, and I worked myself up to a motorman. Now I was really becoming a part of this new journey, and it was getting hard for me every day. One day I decided to go to work on ships, like my uncle and my older brother. I was hitching to port authorities one day when a man pulled over and picked me up. And when I sat down in his car, I heard that voice again: "Here I am." He told me about my life and didn't even know me. He told me to go home and get on my knees, so I dd. From that day on, my life totally changed. I now was almost twenty-one, and I had given my life to the Lord that day. But I was not able to deal with all the new temptations I was around, so I began to go back into the world. I moved in with a woman, and we lived together for six years. One night, on a Saturday, I was stoned on grass, and I was sitting in my

chair, watching a religious program, and I heard the voice: "Here I am, your last call." I lifted my hands up but couldn't move, and I said, "Here I am." I went and woke her up and asked her where she was going to church. I said that morning, "Let's go." So, we went to church. It was my first time since I was that little boy. I went down the aisle and told the pastor I wanted to be baptized. I don't even know why I just obeyed Father.

I went on trying my best to live for the Lord and told the woman we were getting married. So, we were married. She had two children, and now she was pregnant. I was happy but not wanting to have a family. But I had prepared myself in my heart because Jesus was Lord. I went on working and preaching to anyone who would listen. After I was married, it lasted about a year or so, but I took it pretty hard. I came home one day, and she was gone. The next time I saw her I was leaving. I gave her and the children the house and headed to my mom. I had lost my job, my house, and a family. I took care of myself for nine years or so. Even though I never went back to the world, I just did a reset and moved on, and I moved to Dallas. I was now beginning a strong relation with Jesus. He was my Father, and all I wanted to do was to please him. I remember just before I left to go to Dallas, I was to jump out of an airplane. Just before I got on the plane, a girl was making a jump, and watching her fall was not good. Her chute was not opening. She finally pulled the last chord, and it opened. I knew then I wasn't going to jump, so I got ready to go and left. But before I left, I spent some time with my family. Now I was about thirty-two years old and preached to everyone, and of course I was not liked by very many people, even my own family. I was going to move to Dallas and work if I could find a job. It was easy for me now because I had learned many different trades and was working very fast. But I didn't use my trades yet; I just wanted to obey the Lord in whatever I did. Now I was really starting to understand what God was wanting me to see because in the last few years I had begun to doubt who I was. I would try to go to churches, but I just did not fit in until my brother asked me to come to a meeting with him and his wife.

I went and met the pastor, and we became very close. We started a business, and I was able to preach all around. I became a street minister just as I was back home. I took my guitar out that I hadn't played in years and began to play and sing in the church. I was with them for a couple years, and the Lord began to deal with me to come back home. I packed up and hit the road back to the little town where I started and got a job selling campers so I could minister to all the people in the streets. I went to homeless shelters and mission churches, preaching and singing. I was working in the shop when an old friend I knew stop by and asked me to go to New York with him, roofing houses. So, I told my boss I was going, and we headed for New York. We drove straight through about twenty-two hours, and it was rough inside a very small pickup truck. I was able to do my ministry work in the evening, and I met a lot of people. I went downtown Manhattan, and I found a church I had been hearing about and went in. After the service, I went up and met the pastor. He asked me to go outside and walk down the street and tell him what I saw. So, I did, and it was horrible. I have never seen so much evil in one place. I know I was not able to do anything to change it, and he said it would be when Jesus returns. Now it has been more than seven years since my reconciliation, and I was on this journey of seeing life as it really is and a long way from the little town in Texas where I called home.

When we finished the work in New York, I went to Massachusetts and then I was ready to come back home. So, we came home for a week, and I met a young girl who I really liked and would not drive by where she worked without stopping to see her. I had been by myself for a long time, working and ministering, but I had been asking the Lord for someone because I thought I needed a person to be in my life. So about six months after we met, we were married, and everything was good for a couple years, and it began to fall apart. I always had blamed everything or myself until I realized it was a plan that God had to put me through in order to get me ready for what was to come. Just because people are people, selfish, and greedy doesn't make us bad. We are human flesh with the Spirit of the Lord in us to keep us in check and where God wants us to be as his elect. So, no matter what you do or say, it has all been planned out for you, and we can't change the outcome of our journey in this new world.

So now I am again by myself. And even though my life has taken heavy turns, I am steadfast in doing what I was sent on this journey for. Now at thirty-seven, I am a man brought up in morals, ethics, and love. But all around me, in these years, I have seen the awful work against me by the enemy. I was being prepared and armed with power as God gave me in the beginning.

I listened to preachers sang in their church and even preachers attacked me. I have not come back to these churches. I have learned up till now as I always knew as a little boy that I am different and will never be accepted just as Jesus wasn't and how they profess to love him, and they have never known love except for these elect. I am around. I started to work for Oil Co. After I quit roofing, and I have been working since 1988, in 1995, I was learning to fly an airplane because a had a customer who wanted me to fly with him to make my work easier for me. So, I did. One day I was flying across the country, and I ran out of gas. I was not afraid because I knew I was in my Father's hands. I guess it was really hard on my wife at the time because I would be laid up for a while. While I was in the hospital, I was told I had to have reconstructive surgery. But there was a plan in my journey, and it never happened. We think things happen by accident. If that is so, why would God allow us to be hurt and in pain? Because it is his plan for the death of our carnal man, just as Jesus had to suffer for worse, more than anyone has ever suffered. It had to happen. We go through this thinking that God owes us, but in truth, we awe him everything and always never satisfied with what we have and always wanting. We are a nation and a world that hates God and do not even desire to please him. It is a sad thing to see how the so-called church uses my Father. Every day I think back to my times of hearing "here I am" and got stronger as I was tested.

I tell people that I had no reason to ever doubt God in any way. I have tried to use my life before men as my destiny and message.

One day I had a knock on my door, and an officer told me I had to go to court because I had reposed a car that belonged to me. My new journey began—dealing with law and scribes and Pharisees just like Jesus had to do. I was brought to court by my wife's dad who was a pastor who I even helped to build his church. I could not even believe he would say to me and his daughter, "You need to get a divorce." Now this was getting to be pretty hard on me. But when he had me evicted, that was the last a would have to do with him.

These wolves are everywhere, and they have always been here since the beginning. When I experienced the lies and deceptions from so-called churches, I just couldn't take anymore.

I was working one day, and I saw a building for sale, and it was what I was looking for to start a church. I knew of the pastor, so I went by to see him and asked how much, and he told me. I didn't have any money, but I bought it. I got a loan but didn't have money for closing. It was given to me, and I never asked. I didn't quite want to pastor a church, but I thought maybe I might be able to have a real church where the Lord would be truly obeyed and it was going to be a real challenge for me But have pastored the past church in my life, and it was going to be a real challenge for me. I called the building "the church," it was an old missionary Baptist Church and was in good shape. I was able to buy it for thirty-five thousand dollars, and it had an average of land. I had been kicked out of my place now, and I needed a place to live. I put a couch in the sanctuary, and that was where I slept. There was a family next door to my church who brought me food now, and then we would eat out in the little town.. The family was an old gentleman who had five mentally impaired children. The family truly loved me as I did them. They wanted so badly to have a church. So now I knew why I was here, and I would begin to have services on Wednesdays and Sundays, like all religions do. The kids were a great help to me. I began to change the appearance inside, and they would help me to paint and put up curtains to make it look really nice for when we started service.

In 1997, my ex-wife came back to my life. I was in another town, driving in a park, and saw her walking around, holding a baby. I drove up to her and called out, and she ran to her car as if she was afraid of me. I was in my office when I saw her name on my caller ID. So, I knew she wanted to talk to me about something. Of course I had really wanted to know why, but she never called. The Lord had already shown me one night, when I went to see her, and I confronted her, which she denied. The next time I went to see her, I was attacked by the man she had lain with. I couldn't do much of a fight because I had never recovered from the crash and still could not walk without my cane. So, the man kicked me as I was coming down the stairs. But even to this day, I feel so much pain from the deception, but I forgave and moved on. I only can remember the only thing I said to her was, "The Lord will give you a child," and I couldn't because of a vasectomy. So, I think, in her mind, that was all a relationship should be., I guess that is what the world calls the biological clock. I opened the church and had some good and some bad experiences. I sat down, playing and singing one night, and the Lord said, "It is time to move on in this journey." So, I was in Beaumont one day and was waiting with a pastor, and we were talking about feeding and clothing people.

When I was in Austin, I fed and clothed hundreds of people for a couple of years or so. It was great until the local church started to tell me how it should be done.

The phone rang, and it was another pastor. He wanted to buy my building, and he wanted to move in soon. I thought this was great because I could spend more time in the streets, in and around.

So, I met with him. We agreed, and it was done. But he just wanted to let his people know. So, I said fine. He came into my apartment one night and told me he would give me fifty-eight thousand dollars for the building we agreed. The building belonged to the Lord, and I had no 501 c. I never asked a penny from anyone. No one could tell me how to preach. So, I moved in with my mom and took care of her because my stepdad had passed away. Now I had become an old-time preacher in the streets again, and it was great not having to babysit. That's what pastors do. I guess I just spanked the unruly children with the word of the Lord. Having said that, we only hold these offices because we had to be fitly joined together in order to be Christ. But the real problem is the so-called churches. They all think they are the answer. And through my short years, and Jesus said, I will never see my righteous forsaken nor my seed begging for bread. After a little while, I stayed home and sang in a local church. Once the Lord spoke to me and said it was time to move on. My mother asked me if I was leaving. I said, "Yes." She said, "I know, son."

About two or three days later, I looked out the back door, and I saw smoke coming from the direction of the church. It was burning. So, I got in my truck and went there and got my instruments and all the others out. It was bad, and I could hardly breathe. It probably was a dumb thing to do—save someone's stuff—but I did, and he thanked me. I have never gone back to a building again, and I probably never will. I never realized that we have been so deceived by churches and preachers, but here it goes. Even I believed all the lies Satan pulled out, but it took all these years for me to wake from the sleep. But now it was my time.

I was about forty-five or forty-six when I went to Lufkin, and I was hiring people to work for me in the oil business. I hired a young man, and we became friends. Although I never really trusted him, he put a vision in my head to start a restaurant, so I did. Of course, it didn't work out for him because he was not living right, just as I had discerned, and he was letting the business cost me, so I had to take over. I didn't know what to do, but God did. He sent the ones to help me. I made it tell my contract was up, and I shut it down. The word says that you can't serve two masters. It took away from my Father's work. About the time I shut down, we had a bad hurricane come to our town, so I went to try to help people. A friend and old boss had told me he needed me to come and fix the roof destroyed in the storms. Every day I would go and pray for people and help them to get roofs on their houses. In two blocks of one town, there were fifty-four roofs torn off. By this time in my journey, I would have traveled all over the US and even Mexico. I have met a lot of people but not one person like-minded in Christ. I went on for the next few years, seeking the elect of God, and now I was a fruit inspector, as the word says, but not having in success. Now in my fifties, I was beginning to question my reason for still being here. All the years behind me, but I still remember the snake I picked up and my grandfather dying.

This life journey doesn't mean a thing compared to our eternal life that has already been set up. No two people are the same, and that is the way to understand all those around us.

Everyone in their life will have thoughts and doubts of why, and no one has an answer. But my answer is because just and simple because is the reason for my life all I have been through and will go through. It seemed, now in my late fifties, maybe I was alone. But God had another plan for me in this life journey. I saw so much greed and selfishness in people, and it really disturbed me. When I was growing up, everything seemed to be normal. As I get older, things are still the same. All of the racism and hate has just gotten worse, and there seems to be no answer how to stop it. I don't believe that I was everything to be able to change this world, and it was never going to change. I go out in the town, listening, watching, and learning about people and their life. I see much pain in people. There seems to be no joy, and they look so whipped and beaten down.

All these years, I have never found anyone to help me and encourage me about my life, and it has made this journey very rewarding because I never would have gotten where I am. Living in this world always brings up new and different challenges that sometimes we want to give in. But with his plan, we just reset and move for the high calling. I don't really know why it's so much easier if you just relax and let the Lord finish my journey because as I get older now and start thinking about living in this carnal life, it's just not important to me. I am beginning now to relax more and take more and more time talking to people and sharing the Lord's word.

I went to Arkansas today, and I spent time with customers, and I interviewed people to work for me. I am now a regional manager. One young man came, sat down, and poured out his life to me. I asked the man why I should hire him, and he said because he was hungry. So, I knew what it was like to not have anything I hired him, and he said to me, "I will take care of you the rest of your life." I have told this because this now brought me more confidence in him because I knew he was the kind of person I wanted. I see so little love and compassion now, and it seems sometimes I am all alone in this journey. But I know there are others just like me I have been taking care of my ex-wife now for ten or eleven years, just as I did when and while we were married. Today I was told she was going to get married to the little girls' dad, and it was very hurtful. But my Father had all of this planned for me, and I just took it in stride. It didn't last very long, and she asked me to help her again. I did. And as I moved on in this journey, all the hurt and pain was gone.

I am not looking for anyone ever again because it is hard to be with others when you have the mind of Christ. The world now is being set up for the son of perdition, and things are starting to get bad with all the weather changes and signs we are seeing. All the churches are saying Jesus is coming and don't realize he is already here. I was going to move in and start taking care of my mom, so I was not traveling much anymore. My journey was getting closer and closer to coming to so close. A preacher friend of mine stopped by and asked me if I wanted to go to New York with him, and I said yes, and we went in his motor home. On the trip out there, we had a flat tire, and we didn't know how we were going to fix it. We had no spare. So now we were in a mess. We were in Virginia and had nothing for miles. I was praying, and we saw a truck come in behind us. It so happened that the truck was a wrecker.

He said he would take us up in the mountains where he lived. Neither of us was very fine with the idea of being out in this nowhere land. But God's plan was being fulfilled. We got to the man's house, and he said the rim was broken. It was a wheel that was made in France and didn't know we would find one in that country. I looked at him and asked if it could be welded. He said he didn't know. I looked at it, and I said it could be welded, even though I didn't know how long it would hold or if it was possible. We set it up to be welded and put the wheel back on it and drove two hundred miles before we could get someone to look at it. We went on that day to New York with no trouble. It was always worked out by my Father. The next few years were beginning to interest me because I had been through so much the past ten years. The next ten would be an easy ride.

I was getting ready now, thinking about retirement and everyone around me wanted to know when I would retire. I was approaching sixty-two, and the Lord began to really put me through a trial, if I chose to listen to him or others who were telling me to retire. But I couldn't listen anymore to all the babbling from the same miserable soul that tried to turn me to think like mortals other than my Father, so I kept on working in the street, preaching. At that time, I was going to a local police station in the morning and drinking coffee. For the last few years, the force has been increasing my wisdom and knowledge. Now he was giving me the understanding that there was a policeman who I had met in the past, and now he was a chief in the town. In the first year I was around him, I started to really see the person he was. We played guitar. So, when I went to see him, I told him I had a music studio in Beaumont, and he told me he would like to take lessons. So, I asked him to play for me one day, and the Lord started to reveal that he was deceiving me, but I just said, "You play good. You don't need any lessons." So, I would start playing, and I played things he couldn't, so our relation was changing. He saw my Bible and wanted it. I gave it to him, and later I found it covered in junk in his office. He wanted a guitar I had; I gave it to him. After a few months, he brought it back like it wasn't good enough for him. I could go on and on, but I was quick. I knew he was a tormented soul, and I was to move on because he would never let go of himself. I went to him one day and confronted him of his evil ways, and I walked out, and I have never spoken to him again. My love for him was not enough for him, just like Jesus says love one another from the first person in years I was around who I though was of the elect who I have been searching for all my life. But now I know why God had given me understanding and discernment.

Have we ever counted all the cost to follow Jesus? To follow him might mean the loss of something you now hold dear in your like. He said, you who follow me and say that you want to be a man who knows and loves him. I am at this time in my life journey, prepared to take anything that comes my way. I teach truth to those who know me and love me, the elect of God. I still remember, back in time to when I said "here I am, Lord," and my life has never or will it ever be anything but the journey my Father planned out and put into action in 1950 when I was born from the water to spirit soul body. Everything now in my life, all the relations, marriages, sadness, joy, love, and happiness have been temporary, but our lives are eternal. Mom was not doing very good. She had been rejecting me and mean to me when I talked to her about the Lord. She and her sister both attacked me today, calling me a fanatic. But I have had that for years, but now I was sixty-five years old, and I first didn't care what the world thought of me now, what they might say. But I know my mom loves my Lord, so I am not concerned at all about her.

I had to go to the studio in Beaumont the next Monday, and I was there most of the day. But I could not reach my mom on the phone. So, I left to go back to check on her. It took me about an hour. When I got home, the door was open, and my mom was lying on the floor. I could not get her up. She had fallen and broken her hip. Like old people normally are, even me, we want to stay independent as long as we can. I didn't think that this thing called old age would ever get to me, but it is here now, and I will just have to make the best out of it. I had to put my mom in a nursing facility, and it was a hard thing for me to do. But it was for her best because I could not take care of her after that. I just can't forget all the times I had warned her not to do things that would get her hurt and to always use her walker. She never wanted to listen to me, so now she was paying a price for her rebellion. I went every day to see her and make sure she was doing okay. The fall didn't seem to change her attitude at all. But I took everything she threw at me, and it made me stronger. I had to learn through this part of my life to just accept things I cannot change. It seemed, as my knowledge increased, more people came to me and listened. I didn't know if they wanted to understand or just to see. I would handle a situation where I had been ministering to a lot of people in and out of the facility where mom was. I met a couple of guys in the home who were younger than I was, and I helped them get things.

It is a wonderful life when you know the love of God, and that giving and helping others is very crucial on my walk in the life I am in. One of the men lost his home because we had another bad storm, and there was massive flooding. He went with me to look at his house, and he just cried. So, I prayed with him and helped to make him understand why this happened. All during the time I was around this man, I tried to understand and bear with him. One day I went to see Mom, and they told me he had been found dead at his house, lying in the mud. I was shocked and bewildered as to why he would die in such a way. But it was his destiny in this world, and his last journey, and I was a part of him through it. I had been given now a new journey to walk in love and compassion for animals.

All of sudden, after years without anyone in my life, I got a little black dog who just came out of nowhere. I walked outside, and she first melted my heart. I began to talk to her, and now I had someone who I was really learning from. God has given us the animals to teach us what love is and how to be compassionate because we really have never seen true love in this world we live in. I never ever have known the love in this world by people, not even my family. But animals speak straight to my heart from my Father. My ex brought me a puppy she found at her church. So now, in this wonderful life, I have a family that God has sent me. A few weeks later, there was an old dog that came up next door, but the couple next door couldn't keep him. So, she called the pound, and they came out. I ask what they would do to him. They said they would keep him in two weeks, and then they would put him down. I said, "Hell no." You will not give him to me, and he did. Now with three beautiful friends, I was wanting to start a kid's shelter. But it was not part of my destiny, so I let it go. Another dog came up into town, and I tried to find her, but I couldn't. But one might have seen her online on Facebook the next day. I told the mayor to bring her to me. This was her last day to live. She had been there too long. About three weeks later, I got a call from one of the workers in the kennel to come help him. When I got there, he was giving a bath to a little puppy. No one told me he hated his job having to cage these animals, so I told him, "Don't let them go. Freedom to them is the plan God has for them so they can bring joy and happiness to us." All my life, I have loved all animals created by God, even the snake that I picked up when I was three years old.

In all my years in this world, I can't understand why this world of people cannot or will not listen to the Spirit of the Lord. God has given everyone an opportunity to repent and turn from wickedness, but they ignore what he is telling them. Sometimes I even wondered where the elect of God is. All these years of my life, I have decided to seek out only those who have ears to hear and will not cast pearls on these who reject hearing the truth. I realize, I can't be the only one in this world. They were chosen by God to be here in this new life, but it has not been easy to find people who just truly love the Lord more that life itself. All the people in the nursing home are spirits of life gone from them even if they are not sick.

I remember going to hospitals and praying for the people and going room to room and seeing so many sicknesses and diseases and no direction for their life—total brokenness. When we have good health, wealth, and happiness, we forget about the bad times we come through and seek the lusts of this evil world. I think all the people who at the last part in their lives just stop. They reset of their journey, and the Spirit-man begins to take over those who are God's elect to just live in peace, even though the carnal host still lives on. The dead in Christ shall rise because this is their destiny. My mother is coming this her destiny. My mother was coming home today, and she said she was going to listen to me because she had decided it so the way she can stay in for on home. She stayed home a year, and she fell again. This time, she cracked her pelvis, and I had to put her back in. It would work out much better because I just couldn't take care of her by myself. Altogether I took care of my mother for about thirteen years, it was not easy because people at her age want to remain independent, even though they realize their journey is coming to an end. At ninety years old, she had not gotten out of a powerful self-will, not the will of God.

God spoke to me and told me he was going to shake the world and began warning people, but they just didn't believe what is all written in the Word. All the years I have been ministering, I have not seen so many people being deceived by Satan. The people of the land have nothing on their mind but getting an evil man elected to run our country, even though everyone knows how evil the man is and how he has support of all evangelicals in this land. I don't even understand how blind these people are.

It is as though this is their Jesus, and in reality, they have even said this to the world. We are being led by evil, and there seems to be no way to stop him. It is as though he has hypnotized the world to believe all the lies, he has been spewing from his mouth at all those around him save the same spirit. At this point, I was seeing very few people seeking the kingdom of God. I got up this morning and did my exercises, and I looked in the mirror for the first time in a while, and I was looking old. There was nothing I could do. for the first time in my life, I felt helpless because it was finally on this mortal flesh body I am in. There is nothing for me to fear. So even though the change is taking place, the real person who made me is stronger every day, even though the body of flesh is weak. I had been blessed for these sixty-eight years and have remained in a very good, sharp body, mind, and spirit. I knew things were beginning to reshape my journey, so I was studying and getting ready for more complete understanding. To have knowledge, wisdom, and understanding keeps the life sustainable so we are not carried away by winds of doctrine.

Sometimes I wonder what we will do when all the churches are closed down, and people don't have anyone to lead them and tell them how to lead their lives. I have never been one to be led around and told what to do because, in the beginning, I was a leader, and I have always been a leader in everything I have done. In the new world I am in, everything is so chaotic because there are no real leaders because this world is not of my Father, and it never will be. This world is a generation of liars and hypocrites, and they have no desire to change. We should be reaching out to everyone and telling them to repent, even though they will not. I would love to see more people who think like me and could really make a difference in this world. Evil is taking a strong hold on all of our young men and women with all kinds of drugs, and there is no slowing down. I often wonder why my Father has not destroyed all flesh. I was studying in the word, and he showed me in Amos 8 how the great famine in the last days in hearing the word of the Lord. The largest majority of the young people have not even read God's word. All the things that I have been through, I was only able because flesh man dead, and spirit is alive in me forevermore as I live and speak his wonderful word, every moment and breath of this life in this world of evil. I hope that in life, I will always be remembered for my obedience and my disciplined walk with my Father. I have gotten my release from all of my duties as a man of the flesh in this world, and I will walk the rest of my days in spirit and truth.

I never in my whole life on this earth. I'm now approaching sixty-nine years, and the Lord was warning me about judgement on this earth, and his wrath is soon to come for me to prepare. I remember as a young man, God had foretold are they, and we must believe. The life I live is only now, coming on the earth, and we must repent and turn from our wickedness.

I have, for the last years, never seen so much deception in the churches, and now we were seeing all power on high coming to pass. I lived and fought in the first earth age. And now in this second earth age, we will have to fight again, harder than ever. I know, as the Bible says, either we believe, or we don't believe. You can't be on the line. When the spirit allowed me to begin this book, I didn't know what the reason was, but I have done this work in obedience to my Father's words to me to warn those who have ears to hear.

Now is the time to repent, for the kingdom of heaven is at hand. Those who are truly hungry for this wonderful life in this new age, you will have all you need in the word who lives in you, and you shall be filled. Now we are told we are in a pandemic, and it is coming to our land, and it will be like flu. The Lord began to have me to go and warn the people who would listen what was coming, and they just wouldn't listen. I knew it would be a hard task because, all these years, I have tried to reach this land with truth. It seems that as we are getting close to the end of this age of my journey, the word has been heard less and less. I realize everything is going to take place as the Lord has shown me in his words and visions. It was so hard to tell this world that there would be millions to die, and millions would be sick when the leaders of this world would be telling everyone it was going to be okay. I had people tell me I was insane. But now, at this point, there are thousands getting the virus and dying of the disease, and there is no hope in the future for things to get any better. Now the world has turned against each other and is not trying to seek after and repent of this evil they are living in and allowing of destiny them. I don't think even the religious world we have is going to even change its way of thinking and living because their Father is Satan, and this is his world. In my mind and my thoughts and my heart, he says to me, "Through all, here I am. I'll be your shelter from the storm." I was listening to music one day, and I heard a song, and it was called "Here I Am," and I broke down and cried because my Father spoke to me again.

And here I am, and here I'll stay
I will be your shelter
A shelter for your heart
I will be a harbor when the world is cold and dark
I will stand beside you
Through this whole life long
To love you and to give you
Shelter from the storm
The word we never changes.

It says he takes the foolish things to confound the wise. As he spoke through this song, once again it tells me of his love for me.

Now of course it was meant to be a song for a man and woman, but it really showed me what I already knew. God made woman for the man. I really know now why women are what they are. God gave men dominion even over woman, but they had rebelled and turned away from him, seeking after words that tickle their ears. The man has become such an Ahab spirit that women will rule over them. And they know is that they don't have to listen to the man, and they wind up by themselves, pleasing each other, men with men and women with women. The word of God is being stamped out of them because of the flesh not being crucified. I remember in the word where the women gave in to seduction of the flesh. You must realize, everything in this world is being played out the way God said it would, and nothing will change. Man is moving in his greed and selfish ways, just as was spoken, with very little knowledge and wisdom because of his enormous selfish pride, and he will never change. Though all people are going through, very few will seek God as spoken in his word, "Incline thine ears and keep in the midst of thy hearts and it will be health to thy navel and marrow to thy bones." The people of this world seem to think they can go on forever without paying for sin, but they are reaping now, even all the so-called churches who are far from being his bride. Today would be another new beginning in this journey into the realm of eternity, and I would continue to reach out to one more soul.

I went outside and sit in my yard, waiting to see what God would allow me to do next in this wonderful journey. I was starting to feel the age of this life and the pains of my body, but the new man was rising stronger each and every day when the flesh wanted to give in to this life I live. But I would continue on in obedience to the Lord and his next step on the journey of the little boy from a small town. I had been on this journey for about 25,550— days and counting all doesn't mean anything except what I have done by faith pleasing my Father. One day is one thousand years to God, and to try to understand all that I have been through is impossible. In these few years I have on this earth, the only real thing I can remember that I can't ever forget is what I did to please my Father.

I won't ever say it has been easy for me. Even now I have experienced more than I would have imagined. But now things are looking very bad for us because of the pandemic. But I foretold people what would happen. And now it is upon us, worse than man could imagine. But the problem is us. There is no repentance, and I saw one million souls will die in this thing if people don't wake up from their slumber instead of passing the blame on others, not looking at self. People are more concerned about their pleasures than they are lovers of God. I feel deep in my heart for everyone, even those who don't know my Father. For several years, now I have seen so many people with no joy and no emotion for one another. All my life, I have tried to show my Father's love to this world. And just as they rejected him, so did they reject me also.

As I was outside this morning, and I watched the sun come up, a feeling of strength and peace I have never experienced came over me. I have been talking to a lot of people on the phone, and all they talk about is things getting better in this world, and I have to tell them they are wrong. I just don't see very many at all who want to talk about it getting worse. Everyone will bow down and confess Jesus is Lord. The world never has obeyed the Lord, and never will. I think that people should be seeking by studying the word of the Lord. Just today, there were riots and burning of buildings and people being beaten and arrested. We are coming into a time when if you are Black or any color than White, you are rejected, more so than when I grew up in a small town in Texas. I don't know why we can't just love one another and live peace with all man. The problem is deep in the soul of man, and man doesn't want change.

A young man came to see me today and was telling me about his job and what he got paid, and it was very sad to know he wasn't really at peace with his life. He has a good job, makes good money, and things were just not right for him. It seems that no matter what we have in this world, we are not ever going to be satisfied and are always wanting bigger and better. I think back when I couldn't get a job, and I was concerned, but I always believed I was going to be through, and I did. This journey in this life is starting now to be the most joyful time I have ever answered. I know we are getting so close now that every door is being opened. Now my whole life in this world is bringing me to a great understanding of purpose and direction. My purpose is to walk and talk the message all through this land. Now the world is facing just the beginning of what is to happen, and they don't really care. I think now that there will be a remnant coming out of all this turmoil, but not many will change. I have decided to just keep my focus on serving and obeying my Father because there will be those who hear.

I spoke earlier on my story about my wife who now has been around me for twenty-four years but not as wife. She is now, after all these years, seeing that I am called by God as his chosen. He has given her twenty-five years to repent, and now I am beginning to see some fruits in her life. I have lived by myself for all these years and taken care of her and her daughter and other relations I have had. I don't at all think anything is accidental. We have a purpose, and we grow by everything that we go through in this world. Looking back in all those years, I hardly can remember anything about why it all happened the way it did.

A young man came by just the other day, and he was telling me about his job and how he was a college graduate but was not happy because he only made seventy-five thousand dollars a year. His wife made more than him, and they had three little children. I asked him if he ever got to see his family very much, and he said, "Oh yes, I get a few days off on a furlough." I told him that is not good for a family if they expect to stay together. I came to this new world with nothing and grew up all my childhood with everything I needed. And I was content. This forty-year-old man's only focus on life is money. In reality, everyone is the same. He is just starting.

I called the nursing home today to check on my mom, and they said she was fine and seemed to be content. My mom made it through this virus because my Father is keeping his promise to me. I guess in my earthly human mind, I want to see love, but the spirit in me says no but her live her life out for her life journey. Ever since this problem started, I have had so much peace and joy that I just sing and praise and tell my Father how much I love him and want to come home. I love everything that has breath, and I can't hurt any living creature. I accidentally picked up a rock in my yard, and somehow, I killed a lizard, and I just began to cry over the little creature of God.

I have a cat who likes to bring me animals, and I let them go— so far, four snakes, three squirrels, two frogs in about two weeks of the summer. She never hurts anyone of them and lets them go when she sees me. It had been such a learning experience on this journey for me with animals and their unconditional love for me that we mortals just don't understand, nor do we ever want to. I, with my human mind, don't really know about very much at all, but my spirit mind wants to know all things. Have you, for just one moment, ever looked and seen a tree and wondered why there are some bigger than the others, and they can side by side, on how an eagle can fly on above the blue sky? It is a very wonderful and beautiful planet, the world. But evil is everywhere. And now we are in the midst of the coming of the day of the Lord. I don't know how we got to this place in our world, but I do know why. We have always tried to do things our way. Now as we are seeing thousands upon thousands, it is too late to turn back the clock and fix what is broken. We just move on to the next stage of this life's journey for each one of us have again reset our lives and moved on to the next journey. We this journey for me started and wrote my faith says here I am for the last time I will be here doing what he has chosen me to do and fulfill his promise to me. From the little boy who picked up the snake, who saw death for the first time, experienced a formed of human love, to now, I am just now beginning, after all these years, that my life of seventy-one years is a new beginning in this greater part of my life's journey.

As Paul said, the flesh is weak. And every day I get older, I feel pain and hurt. Something never wants to stop. I remember telling people I would never let myself get old. But I couldn't. There is no way to stop this wonderful plan my Father has for me, living my life to the fullest, no matter what I may encounter on my journey. God never said it was going be easy in this world; he simply said he would make a way that no man m. It seems that now I am dealing with people who want to tempt the God whom I love, and I fear but will do them no good. My God is a consuming fire, and he will purge this sinful way of man, and the people have asked me for help all my life, and I have always been a person who gave anything to help. And the most rewarding joy I have received in my life in this new world is being a giver.

One time in my seventy years, I had come to this place of happiness, and I had no one to enjoy my life with because I was closer to obeying my Father throughout this entire journey. As time went on, my life as a mortal seemed less and less important. As Paul said, we die of the flesh and should let go of everything that keeps us from walking in the path God has for us. Life is like vapor; we must live it to the glory of our Father. What is so strange to me is that many people in this world just don't understand when there are more places to go to hear the truth than ever before in time in this world. But scarcely few are going to make it because they are not hearing and don't want to. I know that I have dominion and power in this world, and we, who are his chosen, will tear down everything that is not of God. We walk in power that no mortal can because we were there in the beginning. Mankind doesn't want to, except that we have been here for eternity and will never see death because of our obedience. We see just how easy and gullible mankind is when this country elected pure evil into our house that controls this land we are in. I tried warming, and people made fun of me and still do. Family members won't have anything to do with me. It is so sad how people reject truth, but they have no problem believing lies and deception.

People are getting more and more evil, just like my Father said, and they are not going to change. I realized many years ago that I was to just accept everything that I can't change and live every day to help and love everyone that I can.. I have done the best that I could. I got used to all the hate and death in this new world and have tried to get through just the same. My life has been up to now a rough part of this journey, but my Father just keeps me pressing on for the higher calling in this life. I think when people break all the binders in their life, they will live. We have become simple-minded followers with not very many leaders. I had a conversation with an insurance adjuster and told him he was just a peon, and he got angry with me. I was frustrated with him and told him he was just being controlled. These companies called me every day, trying to sell me things, and it gives me a chance to speak my heart to them and love them. There is no better way to preach to someone except when they are selling you something.

You have someone who will listen to what you say or hang up the phone. I even spend time with people who work for me and teach them things they have never heard of. We are not ready for what is about to happen, so that more people I have the opportunity to reach now as the time. I had the opportunity in the world I was been into to see the richest of the richest and the poorest, and they have no joy because they want instead of give. I learned a lot from my ex-wife whom, after twenty-five years, I still see to her needs. And no matter what happens in my life, I feel I am completely seeing the promises I made when I could not give her a child, which was very hard on her. But I never realized how bad it was until now. During this plague we are going through, she has been there to help me when I need her, even though it costs me things get done I cannot do. I am trying every day to understand her better and try to help her have a good life. I had to learn in my life what I thought was love in my first years. I am trying every day to understand her better and try to help her have a good life.. We make the life in this world by our own decisions, which God will not make for us, even though he already set the plan in place. Everything has consequences in our lives. So, as we move on, we must be sober and vigilant. Sometimes I think about what I would have been like if I had finished school and was able to run and play football, and I just say it's okay.

I have a music studio, and we teach children from three years and up. I have so many beautiful little children that we teach to become great musicians and artists that it fascinates me. I always have loved music and art because it loves us back because of its beauty. I partnered with a young man nine years ago when he came to me for help, and we came together just as God had told me he would reveal those of his elect in this world. I walked away from the responsibility, and he ran everything himself. He is growing by leaps and bounds now, and there is no holding him back. He has become my earthly Timothy, and his love and devotion to me keep me doing what I do every day. Jesus said, "Give me together," and I have asked the Lord the same. We are going through lots of uncertainty in this world, and the journey is getting more and more like I am gaining so much knowledge and understanding. And it is such a powerful feeling. I ask the Lord every day to send someone to me that will have ears to hear. I cannot remember one day in my years in ministry that I didn't pray or talk about my Father, even in my dreams.

I never have ever wanted to do anything in my life but please my Father. I have never understood why. Everyone doesn't feel the same, but it is what it is. I would have gotten into the trap Satan has me up for. I don't know how I would have ever gotten out. Religion and politics have set up this whole world for a total destruction. We are being set up for the wrath of my Father, and the religion and so-called churches don't have any idea what is coming. My God is a consuming fate, and he will purge this earth, just like he did in the first earth age. And the people have never been prepared, only the remnant of God. Those who were there in the first earth age will be saved from God's wrath.

I was always hearing preachers, when I began my walk with God, telling me they would be taken away in a rapture. But when I studied God's word, I never found that to be true, so I tried to make them understand where that came from, and they began to shun me and say all bad things about me. I was singing at a church one night, and the pastor told me he was having an all-night prayer session, and he asked me to come and help him, so I did. And I was talking to some of the women, and they wanted me to explain some things to them about the women Jezebel, so I did. They began to question me about the word and how I know what to say at the right time. I told them it was by spirit, and I left them and came home. A week later, I was to preach in another local church, and I went. When I went in, I went up to sit in the front row, and the pastor came over to me and looked at me with an evil countenance. I had never seen a look like that before in this man. He abruptly asked me to leave. I was not welcome there in his church. I said, "Why? What have I done to you, sir?" He said he was told by the pastor I came to his church and spoke lies to his people, that I was trying to get the women to leave his church. So, I said, "Okay. Goodbye, sir," and I left and never went back again.

So many times, in my journey, I have gone through things like this, but I never gave in to the enemy's flesh because I know what is. In this new life, I have experienced what it is to be just and humble because being humble is walking with integrity and morality, which brings forth faithfulness and kindness and love. I remember one time, as a little boy, when I had my first encounter with a new life and actually saw it happening, as I was riding my bicycle, a little possum had been hit by a car. I stopped to look, and my brother was with me. He said it was dead. I said, "No, there is something moving," and I reached down and pulled a baby from her belly and another and another, until six came from her body. I knew it was meant for me to see that beautiful life come out from death. That is like what happens to us who have been chosen by the Father to receive these powerful moments in life that, at seventy years, I still

see the meaning of it all.

I guess if I could go back in time in this journey to change anything, there is nothing to change. When I started this book, this was to be the first day of the rest of my life. All these pains, feelings, emotions I have written in this book are not just words cast in time, but it is real, and I have lived every moment of it and seen everything I have written because this is what real life is to us in our flesh with the spirit coming forth. The Lord said, "From the abundance of the heart that the mouth speaks," and the words have just flowed through me like rivers of tears and pains of desire, hopelessness, and joy but, above all, a peace within me. There are not enough pages that can really capture my life the real way, only bits and pieces. For nearly two years now, I have been by myself, praying, singing, and glorifying my Father for the wonderful mercy and grace he allowed me. I didn't have any idea how I was going to write this book because I didn't. I just allowed my Father to give me what he wanted me to say. I hope one day that someone will read this life and see that if I survived, then anyone can because you were brought into this world to live in a kingdom of heaven on this earth. When you think about a kingdom in heaven on this earth, what a wonderful place it would be—no sickness, disease, death, hatred, only peace, love, joy, pure and simple happiness. If you could just take time in your mind to let God show you what it would be like to be in his presence, it would strengthen you in every way.

I went outside just before the sun came up and looked up at the sun, and it was beautiful. We have been told in this world that the sun is bad for us. But watch the sun when it rises in the morning, and you will feel energy that will last you all day—only for five minutes. You don't even have to look at it, just let it hit your eyes. Sun warms our bodies. And if you are having pain in your body, get out in the sun, and let the Father heal your body. People come by my house, and they will find me in my chair in my front yard. I was in my chair this morning watching a little bird. I believe it was a mockingbird. I began to whistle with the bird. As I was watching it, I believe it came to me for a reason because there was something about what it was doing. And then I saw it dive down in the shrubs, and a hawk flew down. Then I saw what it was letting me know. I went over and saw a nest in the shrub. How neat that was. But even though the bird was safe, eventually the hawk would prevail because it is my Father way. I raised five dogs, four cats, eight fish, and I have learned to even think like my animals, and my Father even speaks to me through them.

I look up, and I see God. I look down and see my dogs. God and dog— God spelled backward. I get so much love now and joy from just knowing that I am needed and loved in this journey of life set forth for me. I am their protection and covering for their short season in this life journey. Animals are very smart because they are survivors. They know that all it takes to get help from us is their love from the heart of God because he created them for love and companion. I after wonder what would we have ever sense without them and I cannot even be without the unconditional love of them. I awoke this morning, and it was a very stormy morning. There was lightning and thunder. I got up and let my dogs go outside, and they decided for me. They were not about to do it. Even my cats weren't having a good morning. God decided I would go out by myself and see what fear that they were experiencing. I have never in my life had the time to experience such a thing. But when I went out, it had all stopped. It was just raining, and it was beautiful watching God washing the earth. And it was like tears in his eyes. And to say how much he loves me, I didn't feel any fear in the thunder or the lightning. It was like the words I once heard: "Here I am."

I want to someday experience another of those storms just to feel how good it feels to know how much I am loved. I don't think no one really knows the wonderful greatness that our Father has for us, even those of us he has chosen to be in the new age of our journey. I remember that night all over again, how it felt my first time to wake up afraid, and I was so scared something was going to harm me. My mom said, "It's okay. It will let you go in the light. I was never afraid of the dark again, even as a child up till now. I have never been afraid of even death. We just have to accept everything as it may come to our lives throughout this journey.

Now I am trying to understand why so many people are in fear of their lives, but they do not fear God who is a consuming fire. People use my Father's events to the point of abuse like they do a credit card, and it seems that they have no shame or guilt how their disobedience breaks his heart, as those tears, I see from the sky.

How long does this world go on by not obeying God and helping and loving one another before it is too late for us in this life? The clock is ticking, and it is winding down very fast resentence is the only way we will be saved. And even if the word says scarcely, few will be saved in the last days. Last days—that is when the true bride of the Father will fall away from the lies and deceptions that all the so-called churches have been telling them for thousands of years. And then it will be over for the carnal man who has disobeyed God and chased after the lust of flesh, pride of life, and sought often riches that mean nothing to my Father. That little boy who once I knew had polio began to understand and have the mind of Christ. I have received greater understanding because of the work that I did in the first earth age, and now I am bringing forth to life a wake-up call for this land. I see now that if I had never been born into this new age, it would have been such a loss for those who I have had the opportunity to love and help in this new world journey. I understand the manifold mysteries of heaven in this new world that I am in because my Father knew me from the foundation of earth. God said it takes foolish things to confound the wise. In the last few months, we have seen thousands of people die from this plague. Even though there are vaccines to give to the people, there has been no repentance. God said, "If my people who all called by my name will humble themselves and pray, turn from their wickedness, I would hear from heaven and heal the land." But we hear nothing mentioned repentance. I felt so sorry for these sheep who have followed after all these lying and deceiving of so-called preachers because they will stand before God and answer for what they have done.

The very beginning of wisdom is to know God, and you know God through the fear of God. We are just to walk in the awesome power of God who lives forever in us and within us. That is our eternal life; it is for those of this life who just believe. It was hard for me growing up because I didn't have any encouragement for what I could do, just discouragement. When I went to work for my company thirty-five years ago, I was told I would never be able to make a living, and I just wouldn't believe them. I admit I had my doubts about it, but the one thing that kept me going was me. I could go out and brag to those who put me down when I become successful, but I didn't. I won five automobiles and lots of awards for my work, and it was hard. But every day I went out, I prayed for guidance from my Father and stayed in his perfect will. In the thirty-one years I have been on this life journey, I have never missed a meal or a place to lay my head even if just on the ground. My Father made sure I was going to see to it so that I would make it through the journey that he set for me. And now here I am.

Those who have the opportunity will look back and also remember how they were chosen into this world and journey. I know in my heart that God called some of the followers of the life because that is what they were in the first earth age. But also, there are those who are leaders and builders of the works of our Father. You were made differently because of God's purpose and plan for you in your last journey on this earth. You are his chosen, just like me. I know when I first began to reason that I was special, even though I was the only one who believed. Such as rood awaking this world will see when my Father takes control of everything. Every knee shall bow and confess Jesus is Lord, and there will be nothing they can do or say in his mighty presence. Soon he will gather unto him people who of purity. We have trusted him, fought for him, and overcome all the forces that this life journey has thrown at us. The Father said that soon he would gather unto him his chosen army in this world. He has told us that we have to let go of everything we hold dear to follow him. I have prayed all my life on this journey that I would be able to reach just one person for the Lord. And as time has quickly been slipping away, I will continue on, even in this pandemic we are in now because the greatest opportunities in our life always come from tragedy, whether it be good are bad. We are seeing a world we do not know come to pass that even if it were possible, even the very elect will be deceived.. But God's chosen are sealed in our foreheads, which is our mind of Jesus Christ. I don't ever want to

think highly of myself, and I will remain as humble as I have always been. I don't really care anymore what the world says about me because it just doesn't matter.

For this, last year, I have not been able to get out and go very much, but it sure has given me time to reflect over and over again about my life journey and to prepare myself for what is coming. I will not be traveling anymore, so I will not see many people. I think it is time now for me to rest and enjoy the fruits of my labor. In just eight more months of this journey, I will be seventy-one years old, and I feel a lot younger in many ways, but my body is tired. I know no one even wants to admit they are getting old, but mirrors tell the truth. When I was young, I always took care of my body. And the Lord said bodily exercise profits little. And when I was young, I remember how I saw so many people obsessed with their looks and body. And today they just don't look like they once were in the life. It was one thing I never cared to become anything in this world. I have always just wanted to be a person of my own and not be able to fit into the norm of others. I was created just as I am, and I would never change for anyone because I would not be me if I did—the little boy who came into the new journey with only a desire to live. I have been watching for the last few weeks on television how so much hate is being turned loose in this world where people are turning on one another with vengeance. It has always been this way. Except for now, everybody is blaming one another and not admitting we are all the problem. If only we didn't see colors of races and differences in religions and lifestyles, maybe people who truly are walking with God's word really believe love is unconditional. I have seen the dumbest of preachers in my life deceiving and leaving the people, and the people continue to follow them even to their own destruction. There is no way I would ever tell someone that I am a Christian because of how religion has destroyed the name. Man is the great deceiver because man has always been the downfall of every land and is still doing it today. Man has never listened to the Father because he has always done things to please himself. We are not of this world. We are believers. And just as the word says, whoever believes shall have everlasting life. As this flesh is only temporary, we are spirited and everlasting. We will never see death.

The little boy who came home from school that day at recess is the same, and nothing changed but age and body.

I don't know how much longer this world will last nor do I care. And if we involve our minds in this land and the works of the flesh, it takes away from the job that our Father put us here to do. My journey seems to be very short when I look back at my life, and it is compared to eternity. All I want to know is to live and love and serve this land I am in and finish the mission I was called to do in my journey of life. Just imagine what a world would be like without something to hope and pray for and know we are being heard by our Father. All my life in my journey, I have tried to find love in all the human frailties, and there is none without knowing and living in this life without God. One day this land will be gone, but I will live eternally with my Father and those who truly know and understand the awesome unconditional love of God I have been living in this journey of my life. I have never had many on this earth who took time to help me get through the life journey unless I gave them something in return, even though my love was all I was giving. Think how life would be. It would be so sad to not have ever known their unconditional love.

I got a call today from a customer of mine who I have known for thirty- five years and who I first met on my journey. When I went to his home the very first time, he invited me in to sit down and eat with him and his family. Never had that ever happened to me in my life. And every time I went to see him, he would always be kind and loving to me. His wife was a great cook. And if ever I've seen the very first virtues of a woman, I saw one in her. I went by to see him every day. I crashed my airplane, and I asked him to come with me, and he said nope. If God had made me to fly, he would have given me wings.

When God speaks to me, it takes the foolish things to confound the wise. Now that I am older, I can realize and understand the foolish things I have done and why he has allowed me to get this far in my life with very little pain and suffering from those others who don't know him. It is not that everyone is suffering because of disobedience; it is that we're turning farther away from God and seeking pleasure of this world. And what it gives back materializes, which is temporary pleasure. We know there is a great turning away of the church, and it was told to us for our understanding so we would prepare for that is coming. And now that it is on us, there still is no change. We hear the same silly preachers deceiving many, just building up their riches, telling the world how holy they are and how God wants us to supply them with their luxurious I feel so sad for those blinded by the lust of the flesh and pride of this life. They will stand before a consuming fire, and there will be no way for them to escape. I remember back to the first time I preached in a church; I spoke about everything the enemy was doing, and I gave no victory to my Father. Ever since, it has never given any room for him to penetrate my mind, and my thoughts are only of my Father and how he already has defeated him. I don't really know why these people who speak and preach all this foolishness want to follow them other than they followed him first earth age if only in my journey I do anything. I will always speak truth and speak from my heart because from the heart is purity; out of the mouth is power. I look out every day and see such beauty and how we have destroyed it for our lives and comfort. If I had wanted to see something fixed, and I had the power, I would have stopped all the pollution, killing our land and our people. But it had to happen because man got greedier and greedier as the world evolves.

I ask the Lord, "Where are your people? And when are they going to wake from their slumber in this world?" And he said to me from his word, "My people perish for lack of knowledge." You see, people never have wanted knowledge. They just want to control and have power. Now look what it has cost us. I believe the judgment in our land, and it is going to get worse. It is time for God's remnant to come out and encourage one another in the word so we can walk in victory over sin and death. I have been appointed by the Lord, just like each and everyone who are his elect in this new age. It was never hard for me to be obedient to the word of the Lord because he has revealed the manifold mysterious to me, and I know my purpose. I see exactly how this life journey of mine is going through the word of the Lord. I never was a reader or writer, but I have always lived with the word in me. And I couldn't listen to anyone's messages or writing because I never felt the Spirit of the Lord. In these seventy years of my life, I have never once purposed to disobey my Father. I remember when I was a boy, I ran away from home one night because I was going to be spanked by my stepdad, and I stayed outside till my mom coaxed me back into the house. It was very cold outside, and I was glad to get back into the house. A few days later, I was watching my stepdad every night because I knew I had done wrong. He got up out of his chair and didn't say a word to me. He took me by the hand and led me to the bedroom. I got what was coming to me— love a good spanking for cursing him. Never again did I ever even think about a curse coming out of my mouth. And every day we disobey God, it is worse than cursing. We are disrespecting and dishonoring the only one who truly loves us. I hope people will soon wake up and repent of their sins because we are going to see horrible things ahead of us, and I know that my journey is to fulfil the promise I made to my Father when I said, "Here I am." I know in the great land, there are many more of God's elect who have the same sort of destiny, more have waste about in this book. When I sat down that day and began my journey, it had been a wonderful life in this new world, regardless of all the pain and wrong choices, even the many years of being made fun of because I was different. I see children today who are way worse off than I ever was, and they have so much joy because, over the years, there have been so many people standing up for them and helping them. I am very involved in helping everyone, no matter what their situation may be. If everyone learned to be broken and live with a contrite spirit, we would make a great difference in this journey of life and by learning everyone else is more important than we are ourselves.

It seems like since this virus started, people have gotten harder and harder to reach instead of being broken. I would really like to see these last years we have on the journey of life for people to try to learn to love one another the way Jesus had asked us to do so many times instead of dislike and hate. I was working in my yard the other day, and two young men came walking up to my fence and asked me for help. They needed some work, and it so happened I did it. So, I asked them to come back the next day. I wasn't sure they would come, but I felt good about the young men. The one was pretty rough looking, and the other clean cut and very quiet. My flesh was saying they would not come back, but the spirit in me gave me peace. The young men were eighteen or nineteen. Both their mothers and had little infant babies. I thought to myself about my life journey, how I was like those young men but a lot worse. The one really seemed to care about his life and was bound and determined to get through his journey. The other did not. He was a follower and dependent on his older brother to make all the decisions for him. I went back in thoughts of my journey and wondered, What if I would have messed my life up at that age instead pressing on in this journey? They cannot even realize at their age what they are going to have to endure for their journey in this life. The oldest asked me if I was a hippy, and I said I just liked my long hair, and maybe in those days you would have called me a hippy because I looked the part. When I played in their world, I played hard. Being a musician in the '60s, everyone looked like the other. But all through my journey, the Lord has been faithful to me, even through all the mistakes we made. And the young man asks me about his tattoos he had all over him, and I told him, "You aren't perfect, son. You are just forgiven." They came, did the work to ask and talked for a while, and I came back to the house. They came to the door and said, "We are finished. Would you like to check it?" I said no. They never told me what to pay them. As we were talking, they were trying to get their car fixed. I said how much and what was wrong. He told me, "I said I will take care of it," and both men began tearing up and saying thank you. They said they would always be there for me if I needed them. The young man just kept thanking, and I said, "You are my blessing, son." He talked with me about losing four siblings. His mom and dad's use of drugs destroyed and almost got him. He said he had been clean for two years and was never going back. I said, "Talk about children, heads sick, and hearts faint in the last days. They are seed of Satan and born into this world, controlled by those horrible drugs." In my forty- three years in ministry, I have seen so many beautiful babies destroyed by addiction of this rebellion in this new earth age.

The only thing I can see in the spirit for this generation is death and destruction because of rebellion. I am really and truly blessed because God would not let his chosen to get caught in the snare of the enemy. We have been misled all the days of our lives in every way. But those that he has chosen to have been able to blot out everything except the truth. I really feel bad for what I see people are going through. But it's their own doing. The Lord's sheep is waiting to be slaughtered. I have learned in my journey how really evil this world is. It is not the world that is evil; it is the people. But I said this world is evil because it is the people, and they live for nothing. I see what this has done to our children, and they just keep getting worse generation after generation.

When I started this journey, it was as I was, a new beginning to a new end in this life. Even though I have tried to fulfill my life in the way it was planned, my Father knew I would stumble and fall and keep on going to the last breath of my journey. I got a call from my partner at the music studio and began to tell me about something he considered beautiful and amazing. He was walking us to a building, and he saw two little boys about five or six running as hard as they could toward each other. One was Black; the other was White. They ran right into each other's arms and held each other in a loving embrace and would not let even their parents separate them till they were ready. How wonderful those two little boys must have loved each other for them to come together in love like that. A man stopped by today, and we were talking about the virus. I ask him what he thought and if he got shot of the vaccine, and he said yes. This same man, a few weeks earlier, said it was all a lie, and we were being deceived. Then we started to talk about the racism in this land, and he told me in a sharp manner, it has been here all the time. "You are right," I said to him. But does that mean it is the law? In this journey, the life I see in people is a life they actually hate. But they don't know how to break free, so they are so miserable with life. They want to justify this life of sin. We see thousands have died, and this world just doesn't get what my Father is telling them, and they never will as in the days of Noah. At just a turn in their journey, I am really seeing the truth of my life and the fulfilment of the promises. And I don't see those evil people ever desiring to repent and to change.

All through this life, I have been happy even through pain and suffering because I always remember back to why I am here and what my purpose is. And I guess when you have that knowledge, you are special; you have your strength to overcome everything in your life's journey in this world we know is so much evil. And it is because of those who are not obedient to God who are seeking this false pleasure that have been laid out for them. You see when the most powerful people in the world have turned more and more away from God, their lives are in turned. In this age, we seek after things we can't ever get, like the lottery and wealth and power. But we want to make the effort to try to live in this world in peace because of all the lies and deception we are getting all around us in this life. I have now focused on God's elect who, in these last days, will be coming forth as I have been seeing in the last few months. It's time for the new birth to take place on this earth because it is getting near the Lord's return. I know people have been saying it for three thousand years, but it doesn't matter if it is not changing anyone. But if we reach just for the kingdom of God, then we have done what we were to do. Over the years of my journey, I have seen industry, technology, and wealth grow, but more and more people have died because of all this stuff. You might think man would think about the planet more and the lives of the people, but that is just not the case. As I was growing up, you just didn't see all the pollution and refineries that you have today—gambling, casinos, bars, clubs, every dark and evil thing man could think of. And now it all is bringing this world down. Mankind will not ever listen to God because our way of thinking is not the way God thinks. It is so sad today watching all the people lie and continue to lie, knowing God said liars will not enter the kingdom of heaven, and it is just second nature of people. When I told my first lie at seven years old, I will never forget because it did something inside of me that set me free. When we tell a lie, it should break our heart because God hates a liar so bad. I remember the first time I watched television, and I hated it because I couldn't see any good to it at all. I was so sad to see that everyone would spend so much time trying to see something that would not even work half of the time.

Now look where we are today, satellite, computers, and

cellphones, everything that takes our life journey into a tailspin and waiting for what man will do next. We just had a helicopter land on Mars and is taking pictures, and there is really no reason to be on that planet at all. All this great and wonderful wisdom of man is doing is destroying everything he touches, and it is all about to come to a halt. There is one thing we can all be sure of; it is that we all have suffered these last few months in this land because of lack of wisdom of man.

I would like to know what has happened to all the so-called prophets and churches that have fallen in this trap set up for them and all their followers. When the rocks fall, they will hide, and we see it every day ever since this judgment of our land started. And they say it will get worse and worse in the next few months. Every day in the world, I am shown and instructed on what to do each day to be able and be prepared for what is next in my journey in this next step forward. I so hope by all that is happening today that people will start getting ready and, most of all, that they are getting right with God. Everyone has a journey in this world. And even those who are not chosen to a walk like I was doesn't mean they don't have a chance because in Christ all things are possible. I think, if I have learned anything from my journey, it is that we are not perfect. No matter what we think, we are just forgiven. It seems that every day, things are looking bad, just exactly the way I have been told it would be. And I am ready and prepared for whatever may happen. These last few weeks, I have really been put to a test of knowing how to deal with all the people. People are so angry and stressed, and it is very hard not to get myself in the same shape when I get around them. At this point in this life, we are seeing millions of people infected with the virus that I had warmed of, and almost one million souls are dead because of this rebellious generation of people. It seems those of us who are the elect of God are living our life with peace and joy because we know it would be bad in these last days. I think, in reality, we are really seeing the truth of this new age begin to be exposed to what it really is. And even though things will not ever be the same, it is as in the days of Noah, so shall it be again.

I feel so sad to see so many young people on drugs and alcohol, and there seems to be a generation that have not thought of doing good just seeking pleasure in everything but obeying. I can't seem to be able to talk to this generation because of the way they have been brought up in this world. A young woman told me the other day that she had gather a puppy for her daughter, and she won't train or work with it. I said, "How old is your daughter?" She said, "Twelve." And I said, "Does she rule, or do you, her mother?" We have so many kids in our streets today who have not in any way done any better because of the way they were raised. I don't believe we will even get back to a normal life again. And I am telling everyone to get down and pray. It seems this journey I have been seem is coming and is getting closer to a close. I am not and never will be afraid of death. Now do I love this life without my Father who has directed my every path? I would never have believed I would make it. But I knew that if I would keep my eyes on my Father throughout this journey, I would because that was his promise to me. I am really beginning to get tired of the way this people have hurt the heart of God, and they just don't seem to even care about what they are doing. I still am keeping my hopes that there are some who are waking, found their step, and will rise up. I could go on and on and fill in many pages of this book, but the Lord has shown me it is time to close as I approach my seventy-two days on this journey. In reality, one day is as one thousand years to my Father. So, I will live on for many more days till the end of this journey in this second age of time, preparing to be with my Father. Those who read this book are just like me in their journey, even though we have known, but in spirit we are all in Christ Jesus. Amen to this last seventy-one years of this journey and if it were that I would be here another few years before the master comes and takes me.

I thought I was almost to close out this book I am writing, but God has a different plan. Even though I am getting tired of reaching out to the lost souls of this world, and age is catching up on me in this body, it's as though I am renewing and even getting stronger. And my spirit man is rising up every day and keeping me on this life journey. As Paul said, the flesh is weak, but the spirit is strong. They are saying now how things are getting better even in a year of lockdowns, but I know better because the word of the Lord says, in the last days perilous times will come, and we haven't seen anything yet. And even though times have been different, they are not over by now. It means until the return of my Father, just as he faces told us in his word. I am to consume my time in his word because it is so important now as we are coming to a close in this earth age, and it is just around the corner for us all. God's elects are ready and have been ready since the beginning of the first earth age. What has been exciting about my life as I have lived is everything, I have been told to me by my Father is being completed. It seems as though I have been living in a dream, and now it is all becoming reality to me. I have very little time now to get this word out to this generation of lost souls. There are so many different churches and doctrines in the world, deceiving and confusing people that they don't know where to go. Sometimes it seems that I just get tired of dealing with people, but I just go to the word and build up my strength to move on. The more I ask for knowledge and wisdom, the more the Father requires of me; so, I have to get ready because it is not going to be easy for us from now on. But everything is counted as joy. In this life, people are in so much pain and suffering, and it is going to get worse. If the people would return to the Father, it would give them all the strength they need in order to go on. I have not been able to in all my years. It seems that people who were brought up in these churches are not able to carry on with their lives and sin with no repentance.

If all of the people in my life's journey that I have heard of were saved, why is our world in such shape as it is? Jesus said, "You knew me not workers of you sins and deception, lies, iniquities." Time has almost run out in this world for the hearing of the word of the Lord. When you see families being ripped apart and divided because of politics and religion, you have to realize we are there. In forty-five years of my life, preachers have disgusted me to the point that I will not listen to any of them. They are robbers and beggars, and God will not tolerate it in any way. The great shaking is here, and it will be devastating to this world. If it were possible, even the very elect would be deceived in the last days. This is all happening to wake the elect and to prepare for this new age war we are about to go through. I was told of everything happening all my life, and I now have been as good a watchman as I know how to be. And you know, one really believes until it happens to you. Right now, over seven hundred thousand people have lied, and it will be many more if God's people, his elect, will rise up and speak to this would of evils. All I hear is about politics and the economy, and lives are not changing. For a while, there has been a beautiful peace all around. But human flesh has to have more excitement, lust, pride, and they are going right back to the evil days we came from. I suggest that the best thing we can do is to stay in the word of the Lord because it is going to be a rough road ahead for those who are in disobedience. I hope by me writing this book about my journey, it will somehow reach those who are really listening to what our real purpose on this earth has always been. And wake up because Jesus is saying in these last days, "Here I am, the beginning and the end."

ABOUT THE AUTHOR

I am now approaching seventy-two years old in this world, and I have experienced a lot of life that there are not enough pages to put in a book. But this book is me and my experiences—a life of joy, sadness, and grace. For me to sit down and write a book was very new to me, and I didn't really know how until my Father said to me, "Here I am," and then I knew it was to be done. As the words came into my mind, my heart came out to express every thought I had in me. I am the same every day of my life as I was as that little boy who first heard those words, "Here I am."

www.ingramcontent.com/pod-product-compliance
Lightning Source LLC
Chambersburg PA
CBHW051649120626
46551CB00015B/2277